Portraits and Dreams

Photographs and stories by children of the Appalachians

Wendy Ewald

Introduction by
Robert Coles

Afterword by
Ben Lifson

Writers and Readers Publishing, Incorporated

Writers and Readers
Publishing Cooperative Society Limited
144 Camden High Street
London NW1 ONE U.K.

Writers and Readers Publishing, Incorporated
500 Fifth Avenue, New York, NY 10110

Portraits and Dreams
Photographs and Stories
by Children of the Appalachians

First Published by
  Writers and Readers Publishing, Inc. 1985

ISBN 0 86316 087 5
ISBN 0 86316 088 3 paper edition
1 2 3 4 5 6 7 8 9 0

Manufactured in the United States of America

page 1:
Fourth grader
My family on Cowan Creek

page 2:
Allen Shepherd
Lee Allen on the painted rock in his grandmother's yard

opposite:
Ruby Cornett
Jep and Wee's farm at Haillie

The publication of this book and the photography workshops from which the material
was collected were funded in part by grants
from the National Endowment for the Arts,
a Federal Agency, the Polaroid Foundation,
the Kentucky Arts Commission, the Public
Welfare Foundation, and the H. T. Ewald
Foundation.

This book is co-published by Appalshop, Inc.,
a non-profit media collective.

  The children's photography project is part
of Appalshop, a community cultural center
for central Appalachia. The other parts of
the Appalshop are Appalshop Films, June
Appal Recordings, Roadside Theater, Head-
waters Television and WMMT Radio. For
more information write Box 743, Whites-
burg, Kentucky 41858.

Dedication
For my teachers, Piola Terry and Wendy MacNeil, and for my students and their families on Campbells Branch and Cowan and Kingdom Come creeks.

Acknowledgments

I wish to thank Bob Gatton, Shelby Watts, and David Chaltes for making it possible for me to work in the Letcher County school system, and Marnie Samuelson and Marcia Schiff of the Polaroid Foundation, Jon Dunn and Nancy Carpenter of the Kentucky Arts Commission and my father, H.T. Ewald, for their continued financial and emotional support. I am especially grateful to Liz Barret, Glendora Halcomb and Darlene Dixon, who were my co-teachers, for their indispensable collaboration, to Katy Homans, Patt Blue, Dee Davis, Jane Gianvito, Joe Gray, Ben Lifson, Glenn Thompson, Tom McDonough and Wendy MacNeil for their valuable insights which guided me in putting together this book, and to Robert Coles for his generous introduction.

Contents

Ruby Cornett
Up Big Branch from my front yard

Introduction

Robert Coles

In 1965, when I began working with Appalachian children in West Virginia
and eastern Kentucky, I found myself in a quandary of sorts. I'd been
reading books about the region, mostly by social scientists, and had
learned from them about its remoteness and about the consequences of
that geographic fact – the psychological remoteness of the people who live
up the hollows. At a conference I attended in Lexington, Kentucky, "The
Psychology of Appalachia" was discussed at great length. By then I'd put
in a few months of trudging up and down hollow roads and was as
perplexed as I'd ever been. How to reconcile, I wondered, the kindness and
courtesy and, yes, the eager openness of the families I was visiting with
the descriptions of people I was hearing at that conference and had been
reading in all those big-deal books?

Eventually I began to relax with the boys and girls I was meeting,
with their parents and teachers – and let the truth of their lives stand on
its own: their everyday habits and customs, their spoken thoughts, their
pleasures and worries put into action, a collective truth easily the match of
that offered by any "expert," whatever his or her academic credentials.
But books, too, can respond to this life's rhythms, capture them, do them
justice, do them proud – and none has yet done so better than this one. It
is full of the many truths the region's children have to offer – rendered
through their voices, their vision given expression through the magic of
camera film.

Again and again these young people let the rest of us know how hard
their life may be, yet how hopeful and thoughtful they are, how determined
they are to get on with it, do their very best, acquit themselves decently,
no matter the constraints, the jeopardy a given fate has bequeathed them.
There is an early stoicism here, but also a substantial joy in the modest
offerings. There is, too, an immeasurable dignity – that of children brought
up to bow before luck, good and bad, before circumstances, favorable or
quite limiting, and not least, before Almighty God, whose presence in
many of these lives can often be felt, rather than known because of words
spoken or churches visited. (Not that there isn't plenty of churchgoing!)

As I looked at these pictures and read the text, I was carried back to
my own working days in Appalachia and reminded, yet again, how
fortunate this nation is to have in its midst such lively, thoughtful,
thoroughly decent children, capable of the innocence and exuberance of
their age but also of a deepness, an earnestness, a wry and gentle humor,

courtesy of Wendy Ewald's knowing, sensitive, patient, dedicated attentiveness to them. Hers is a special task, a modest one, indeed, that of the intermediary between a "them" and an "us," the readers. She has done her job with brilliant success, and the result is a fine, fine book – words and pictures aplenty to cause in us wonder and delight and even a touch of awe. Here are our young fellow citizens, as the saying goes up those hills, "from yonder," to give us their ideals, their preoccupations, their visionary moments – in sum, their haunting, touching presence. Our response, no doubt, will be one of acknowledged edification – much learned; but one hopes and prays that that response will include a moment of thanks to the teacher, Wendy Ewald, who has helped these younger teachers, these Appalachian boys and girls, educate us strangers to their land and life.

Preface

Wendy Ewald

In the communities of Appalachia, where few extra material comforts exist, photographs are startingly prominent on the walls in people's homes and in family albums tucked away in living-room drawers: photographs of schoolchildren with brushed hair and buttoned collars; young men in army uniforms; families grouped around the casket of a relative or a friend; photographs telling the stories of the families who live there, binding the generations and preserving the past.

Perhaps it is this familiarity with photographs that explains why these photographs made by children in Kentucky are so extraordinary. But the children were already keen observers. Their parents taught them respect for and fear of their surroundings. They watch the crops grow, the seasons change, the animals being born and slaughtered, and when the boys go hunting they sit quietly watching and listening for signs of nearby animals. Their photographs speak from within their lives and record moments that suggest rhythms of everyday life. The world they present is small and intimate, but their perception of it is detailed, accepting and complex.

Although much has changed during the last generation, life on Cowan and Kingdom Come creeks and Campbells Branch is still intimate, quiet and strongly independent. Ties to the land, families and community are closely held, rooted in a cultural past and bound to nature's rhythms of birth, growth and decay. Most families tend gardens and keep a few animals. Coal mining is just about the only outside employment. Each town has a post office that is also a general store, a church and a school.

The photographs in this book were made by students of the three schools in these southeastern Kentucky communities. They were chosen from the work of 150 children between the ages of six and fourteen. The words are from conversations I had with eight students who were eleven, twelve and thirteen.

I arrived in Kentucky in February of 1975. I was twenty-four and just out of college. I rented a small house on Ingram's Creek, one of the most remote and beautiful hollers in Letcher County. I wanted to make a document of my new community that had the soul and rhythm of the place, but the camera seemed to get in the way. I also wanted to get to know the people, and the one thing I could offer them was to teach their children to take pictures. I had taught photography to Indian children during my summers in college, so after a month of settling in and meeting my

Lee Allen's grandmother's frame of photographs
Wendy Ewald

neighbors I decided again to teach students in the local elementary
schools. I had heard that the principal of Cowan Elementary School,
Mr. Gatton, might be receptive to my idea. I went to his office one day in
March and left a message with the secretary. Within half an hour he had
tracked me down and was ready to begin. A grant from the Polaroid
Foundation provided us with cameras and film. That April I taught a class
for the fifth, sixth, seventh and eighth graders at Cowan and in May for all
the students at the Kingdom Come School. Because of the success of this
small project, the next year the Kentucky Arts Commission gave us
darkroom equipment and a grant for supplies.

 During the next school year, 1975–76, I taught in three schools. We
built darkrooms at the two larger ones – Campbells Branch and Cowan. At
Cowan all that was available was the boiler room. The furnace was fired by
coal and when it kicked on I had to yell to be heard over the roar. We ran
hoses along the floor from the water tanks to mix chemicals and wash
negatives, but sometimes they broke and the coal dust and water mixed
together to leave a layer of gray sludge on the floor. We put our four new
enlargers and the stabilizer that develops, fixes and spits out a dry print in
ten seconds in the janitor's closet. Half of the students could print in the

closet while the other half developed negatives in changing bags in the boiler room.

Once we had built the darkroom we began using Instamatic cameras, which gave us negatives. Each student bought a ten-dollar camera from me; I hoped that by buying the camera he would value it as something he had worked for and would have as long as he took care of it. If he didn't have the money, he earned it by mowing lawns, or holding a bake sale or a raffle. I supplied the students with film and flash.

Like any artists, they were inspired sometimes more than others. They needed to have their cameras with them always and plenty of film, so that when they wanted to photograph something – a hog killing, a colt being born, a birthday party – they could. For the best of them picture taking became, simply, part of their lives and especially of their play. Kingdom Come was one of the last one-room schools in Kentucky. It survived consolidation because the buses couldn't bring children down the road out of the holler to school. The road in a few spots is actually the creek. The school building was a white wooden house on the land that had been given to the county a hundred years ago by the Ison family. Before the roads were built and cars were available the school had maybe a hundred students. When I arrived there were only seventeen. Inside were two big rooms, the kitchen and schoolroom. Every morning during the cold months the students took turns bringing in coal from the coal pile next to the creek to fill the potbellied stove that heated the school. They studied together in small groups: Freddy Childers and Billy Dean Ison in the first grade and Shirley Couch in the second grade, Amy Cornett, Mary Joe Cornett and Tammy Williams in the third and fourth grades. The older children helped the younger ones.

The first day, I gave out the Polaroid cameras and showed them how to set the distance, to push the shutter without moving the camera, how to pull the film out and coat the picture. Each student took one photograph while the rest of us watched to catch his mistakes. Freddy was by far the smallest, shortest kid in the school and the most energetic. He was called Kojak because his head had been shaved to get rid of lice. He took his first picture of Billy Dean, who was at least a head taller. He didn't understand that he had to change the angle of the camera in order to include what was above or below his eye level, so Billy Dean's head was cut off. The other students made fun of Freddy but then explained that only what was inside the white line painted in the viewfinder appeared in the photograph. He caught on, and the first time he took the camera home brought back two self-portraits: "Me and my brother Homer" and "Self-portrait with the picture of my biggest brother, Everett, who killed himself when he came back from Vietnam." In his portrait Freddy holds a picture of Everett when he was a boy. Everett had been the favorite son. One day after he came home from Vietnam he put on his army uniform, turned on the radio, and shot himself through the heart. Homer is Freddy's retarded brother. His speech is slurred but Freddy understands him and takes care of him as

Wendy Ewald helping Lee Allen Carver lay out his book
Rick Bell

Fifth graders at Campbells Branch working on
a preliminary layout of the book
Wendy Ewald

if he were his little brother. Freddy kept Homer in cigarettes, which he
had a habit of eating, and made sure he didn't wander off. He never
thought to be ashamed of Homer.

Bonnie and Luke Capps are twins. Bonnie was in the fifth grade and
Luke in the fourth. They both loved to photograph their flaxen-haired half-
sisters playing in the mud or on their bikes in the afternoon. Mary Joe
Cornett was a shy girl in the fourth grade who didn't hesitate to direct her
subjects with authority. The photographs of her family are carefully staged
portraits at mealtime, in the barn or in front of old family portraits.

In the Autumn of 1977 I taught the fourth-grade class at Campbells
Branch. I had been warned by their teacher that these children had the
lowest IQs of any in the school. As it turned out, they were the most
talented group I worked with. The first day, their teacher sent them to me
single-file. Billy Jean Ison, Robert Dean Smith, Maywood Campbell, Ruby
Cornett and Greg Cornett. I realized that except for Denise Dixon and
Myra Campbell, who were extremely skinny, all were short and fat. Their
teacher had also warned me that they were rowdy, but I found them to be
so well behaved that I wondered whether we could relax enough to work
together. Once they took the cameras home and developed their first roll of
film, they were so excited they forgot the rules of formal classroom
behavior. Instead of taking their seats and waiting for instructions as they
did in their regular classes, they began to work right away on their own.
Some would help me set up – sweep the floor, clean the drying cabinet.
Ruby, Denise and sometimes Johnny Wilder mixed the developer, while the
other students developed film or began printing. Now in order to get their
attention I had to call a group meeting. They were independent and
passionate workers.

Darlene Dixon, a teacher's aide, watched over the darkroom, and I
stayed outside to look at the contact sheets and prints. Every semester
after a conversation with each student about what he liked taking pictures
of and what his problems were I made suggestions about what he might

Campbells Branch photography students
Wendy Ewald

try next. I noticed that Maywood Campbell's pictures were always slightly disappointing to her. I looked at her negatives. She had chosen to photograph very intimate family moments, but her compositions were a bit off. In one photograph her little brother was riding on her grandfather's shoulders. Their outstretched left arms were cut off. She had tried to center her compositions, so they fell apart when she didn't succeed. I advised her to walk around and just look through the camera for a few days to become more aware of the edges of the frame.

I wanted to create a lively, open atmosphere in the classroom so the students felt at home expressing themselves. There were materials for drawing, writing and making books, and there were always photography books. The pictures were starting points for all sorts of conversations. Allen Shepherd and Robert Dean picked up a book of photographs of World War II. Their reactions drew the others. "Man, look at these." We sat on the floor around the book and I asked them to tell me what was happening in the pictures. When they looked at a photograph of Hitler, I asked if they

Denise Dixon taking a self-portrait
Wendy Ewald

Denise Dixon posing her twin brothers
Wendy Ewald

knew who he was. "A baseball player," Allen guessed. I was startled that they had never learned who Hitler was, so I told them what I knew about Hitler's role in the war. Then we looked at the picture again. I suggested that what we know about the subject of a photograph changes our interpretation of it, but it should contain clues that point us in the right direction.

I also brought in books made by other children, some of them diaries published when their authors were adults. *Opal* is one begun by a country girl when she was five. It describes her fantasy world in the country. We took turns reading it out loud, and Billy Jean and Allen literally fell off their seats laughing about the "cathedral service" Opal held for her pig Aphrodite. Reading Opal's stories gave them the idea that other children could enjoy their pictures just as much as they had Opal's stories. Her diary encouraged some of them to write. Robert Dean kept a diary for a year. For the first month I could not read a thing he had written. There were no spaces between the words and he had spelled everything phonetically. When I deciphered it, I found that he had written beautiful passages each day about what he had done, what his hounds had tracked or how the corn field looked in the afternoon.

Persuading them to see the eloquence of their rough photographs was more difficult. There were no books of children's photographs to look at. They hadn't seen anything like the photographs they were going to take in subject matter, tonal range or surface. The portraits they admired were the portraits of Hank Williams and Dolly Parton on their album covers and the landscape pictures of fields of flowers in the seed catalogues, but they were able to give each other encouragement. Almost every day they put up

Denise Dixon photographing her twin brothers
Wendy Ewald

their pictures for a discussion. I guided each one to tell us what he was trying to say with his pictures and the others to tell him what feelings the pictures evoked for them. In that way they could learn to communicate first with each other. Later, when they had exhibitions in the school, in the town bank, at the University of Kentucky and finally in galleries in New York and Chicago, they could see the value of their photographs in other contexts.

As they became more comfortable with the camera, I wanted them to expand their ideas about picture making but to stay close to what they felt deeply. I asked them to photograph themselves, their families, their animals, their community, stories they could tell with pictures and finally their dreams or fantasies. When they made self-portraits they learned that they could be the subjects of their own photographs and create characters for themselves. The assignment to photograph their dreams brought into play their imaginary world. Before they began, to establish a receptive audience for their very personal and often frightening fantasies, we closed ourselves in the darkroom, sat on the floor and told each other our scariest dreams. The photographs they took afterward broke new ground for many of them. They saw they could produce whatever image they wanted. Scott Huff hadn't had any luck with his pictures until then, but he strode into my room triumphant with his roll of dream pictures. He told me they would be good if he could develop them right. His hands trembled as he agitated the developing tank, but he had no problems, and a fine series of pictures – "A flying dream" – resulted. Allen Shepherd had a fight with his best friend, Ricky Dixon. He and Ricky had swapped knives and Allen felt he'd been shortchanged. They weren't speaking to each other until one night Allen

Russell Akeman taking a family portrait   Russell Akeman taking a self-portrait in front of the barn
Wendy Ewald   *Wendy Ewald*

had a dream that he'd killed Ricky. He decided to make a photograph of
Ricky dead in the forks of a tree. He asked Ricky to pose for him, and
during the making of the photograph the two boys made up.

Others didn't need such urging to experiment. Denise Dixon and
Russell Akeman loved to take pictures. Russell lived with his grandmother,
brother and sister. He wanted to be a photographer and was encouraged
that there was a famous photographer named Russell Lee. Russell's
subject matter was limited to himself, his animals and family, but his
enthusiasm led him to an understanding of photography beyond most of the
other students'. His grandmother's farm sits below the road in a little holler
of its own. There are lots of animals around – chickens, ducks, a horse,
cows and pigs. It is an old-time farm that still looks like it was carved out
of a wilderness. It has been kept with such care for generations that the
way the fields are laid out, where the lawn ornaments are placed and how
the outbuildings have been mended are all part of the nature that
surrounds the neat white wooden house. The compositions of Russell's
photographs sometimes mirror the natural balance and playfulness of the
landscape of his grandmother's little holler.

You can see in Denise's photographs that she was a beautiful ten-year-
old. She was the best dressed and most ladylike of the girls in her class.
With the first roll of film she took I noticed that she had a distinctive and
original sense of composition, and she never ran out of ideas as some of the
others did. I visited her at home several times. She had set up her room as
an oversized doll house with stark white walls and a few posters of animals
and family portraits. She created tableaux with her dolls on the bureau,
night table and bed, and likewise in her photographs she made up fantasies

Russell Akeman photographing his brother
Wendy Ewald

involving her twin brothers, Phillip and Jamie. Her careful arrangement of
her room and her dress was similar to the care she took in the composition
of her photographs. When I asked her to document her Thanksgiving
dinner, she took a picture of the turkey on a plate on the bare formica
table. As with her room she included only what was essential.

Denise worked with me from the fourth through the sixth grade. In
the seventh grade she became a cheerleader and basketball player. She
wore makeup and flirted with the boys in the eighth grade. She took fewer
pictures and finally told me she wanted to quit photography class. She had
lost her interest but couldn't explain why.

Russell started taking pictures when he was in the fourth grade and
didn't stop until the summer after the seventh grade. He grew a lot during
the summer and his voice changed. I taught him how to use a 2¼ twin lens
reflex camera to try to renew his interest, but he began skipping
photography class. He would say "I'll come in a minute" and never show
up, or if I went to his room to look for one of his classmates he would avoid
my gaze. I suspect he didn't like the attention, which earlier he had
sought, that he got from me or from his pictures. His ambition to be a
photographer I think seemed childish to him now. He knew it was more
likely that he would be a coal miner.

I had fallen in love with Russell and Denise during those years. They
were my companions. Once Denise and I stretched out on her bed and
talked for hours about her dreams and premonitions. Russell and I
photographed together at his grandmother's house. A couple of times I
held my breath as I watched him climb to the roof of the barn to take a
picture with my Hasselblad. We were like accomplices in a secret game.

We knew as photographers that we sometimes had to trick the adults into letting us take the pictures we wanted. It may have been love that propelled them to photograph in relationship to other forms of love in their lives, but when they reached puberty they grew up. They became mountain men and women with the limitations and protection of their society. Amy Cornett quit school and married Billy Caudill. Luke Capps joined the army, and Bonnie, who wanted to be a lawyer, is a waitress at the Pizza Hut.

I couldn't push Denise or Russell to continue. I realized I was trying to hold on to a period of their lives that they had let go of. Their eloquence with the camera was a passage of childhood. They would have to become conscious of their natural abilities and become photographers if they were to go beyond the point they had reached. Maybe at some other time they will pick up a camera again or express themselves in another way. Their pictures are in their family albums or pasted on the wall, mixed in with the pictures taken by their parents or by the studio photographer at the dime store. Junior Childers came by the other week with his new wife to show her the darkroom and tell her about the time they used to take pictures.

Self-Portraits

Albert Ison
Self-portrait with my .22

Allen Shepherd

The mountains—I feel they have secrets like nobody has ever heard of. Some people say if they could talk they would speak wisdom. I feel that way too.

I guess I've been in the mountains so much, it just makes me feel like myself. I listen to the birds, hear the hawks and crows. Hear the squirrels a cutting and a hollering. It smells fresh. There isn't anything there that can bother you lessen it's a snake, and if you don't get around one, it won't bother you. When I'm mad and go out into the mountains, it makes me get over it.

I had a lot of fun when I was little, a lot of fun. We used to pull off all our clothes and get in the creek and play. Mom didn't know where we were. She would holler for us all day. We'd go and catch crawfish and put them on mom and she'd whoop.

In ten or twenty years things will change here maybe back like it was in the old days. We'll ride horses and carry big 45s on our sides. There won't be much money. We'll run out of coal and gas, but it'll give the mountains time to settle back down and grow trees.

In ten years, if there's any coal left, I'd say there will be five or ten boys out of my classroom working in the coal mines. The girls will probably sit back and watch the men work. I don't believe I'd like to get married. Maybe when I get about 40 or 50 I might, but I'd want to marry someone that loved me. I don't know what kind of girl I'd like to marry—I haven't seen 'em all yet, but she'd have to be something like my mother. And if we had kids, I'd want my kids to get out there and play. Be like kids oughta be.

My father worked in the coal mines. He ran a shuttle car. He ran a loader and a roof bolter. I guess he liked it. He worked about eighteen years. He stopped because that lung of his collapsed because of coal dust. It got in his lungs and hardened just like a rock. It looked right white looking in his lungs. That's what the x-rays showed up on Daddy. He coughed all the time, and he still does. He started working when he was about eighteen and quit when he was about thirty-six. Now he sits around the house. He wishes that he was out working. Me and him go squirrel hunting sometimes. I remember him coming home from work. He used to bring us chewing gum in his lunch bucket, and his face was all black.

Three of my uncles still work in the coal mines. One is a boss. One drives a shuttle car, and the other one runs the bolting machine. One of them has heart trouble. Another one got his skull busted. A rock fell on him and his knee was crushed. He can't work and they won't give him social security. I'd say it would be all right working in the coal mines, if you liked it, but if you didn't it would be hard on you. They say that's the darkest dark you've ever seen down there.

I'm not scared of dying. Everybody's got to die sometime. I'm just afraid of suffering. Old Carlos Watts that lived up above me here, he died the first day of January. He died of cancer of the pancreas. All his hair came out. They say he went down until he weighed 90 pounds. You know a grown man about fifty years old is pretty good size, but he looked just like a little kid laying there.

Carlos's wake was scary. When we got up there to where he was laid out, it was night and just about everybody had gone to sleep. I was outside. I didn't want to go in the house. What if his spirit had come out, while I was inside? I wonder what it would have looked like? It would surprise you wouldn't it? It would be just like you knew that there was a Jesus Christ and he was coming back for you someday.

Russell Akeman
I am lying on the back of my old horse

Russell Akeman
I am lying on the back of my old horse

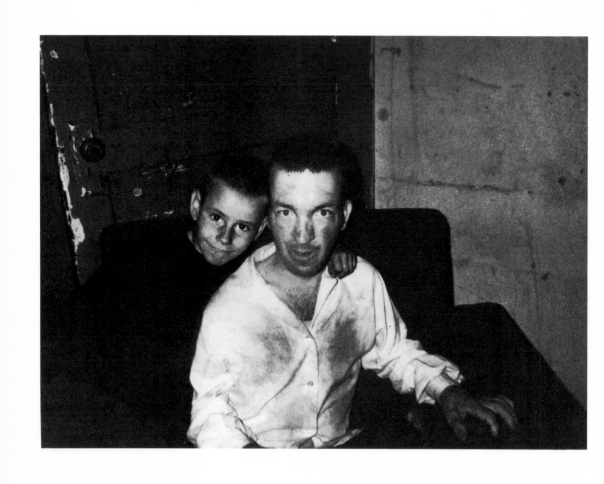

Freddy Childers
My brother Homer and me at our house on Kingdom Come Creek

26

Freddy Childers
Self-portrait with the picture of my biggest brother, Everett,
who killed himself when he came back from Vietnam

Billy Dean Ison
A picture of myself with the hounds

Robert Dean Smith

I favor my dad, but I act just like myself. I'm sort of tall and fat. I'm almost as tall as my dad is, but I'm taller than mom. I lose my temper a lot. When anybody makes me mad, I'm ready to fight.

There are times things come into my mind and I remember them, and times when they won't. Now I've been told this. I can't remember it, but when I was two years old, I'd eat red worms out of the yard and wouldn't wear a diaper or anything like that. I'd get out in the chicken lot and go get the eggs. I was wild. I played cowboys and Indians—Daniel Boone. Now I can remember that well. I'd wallow around the floor by myself just fighting an imaginary person. My dad said they used to play in an old buckeye tree. One of them played the hunter and the other one played the squirrel. The one who was playing the squirrel got up in the buckeye tree, and the other would shoot at him, make him fall on his head. Just play.

My house is white. It's got two stoves in it. Part of the yard is green. The house has three bedrooms, a kitchen, and living room and two porches. It's all right. I like where it is—up in the holler where it's peaceful. There's nobody to bother you. We're five hundred feet from the nearest neighbor, and they don't make any noise. When I look straight ahead from the house, all I can see is trees and the road, and the land is good soil for tending gardens.

Fall and spring are my favorite seasons. In the spring, it's green and beautiful out. In the fall the leaves fall and the cool wind blows. It's just a good feeling to get out and get around. Spring time makes you just want to slob up in the sun on the side of a hill.

When I get older, I'd like to live in the same holler. I know that. It's just a peaceful place. I'd build a cabin somewhere and live in it. I'll probably follow after dad. I'll work in the coal mines and just live right there.

My dad's a short skinny fellow, all the time joking around, but when you make him mad, he usually uses a shot gun. He doesn't bother anybody else and he doesn't like for anyone to bother him. When they do, they have a war on their hands.

He draws unemployment and stays around the house. He has black lung. It makes him wheeze and cough and short of breath. He stopped working in the mines a year ago. It makes me feel better for him to be at home. We go hunting, fool around the house, build stuff. I learn plenty of things.

My grandfather draws black lung. He sits with his nose over the stove and sniffs ashes and growls about the money he spends. Sometimes I walk over and stay with him about a week. It's not far. I just have to cross one mountain. He wants me to stay right on, but he knows I can't do that.

Denise Collins
Self-portrait in front of the mountain at sundown

Darlene Watts

When you're in love you do funny things like lay your books in the refrigerator. I think it sounds nice, but when it comes to marrying, I don't know. Marriage seems to suit everyone else. In some ways, I guess it would suit me too, but I worry that I won't be able to get along with my husband—not suit him. I'd like to have a perfect marriage, but that's hard to come by these days. I know one thing, when you get married, you can't lay your books in the refrigerator any more because your husband would get mad. He usually acts like he's the boss, and I don't like anyone to boss me around all the time. Sometimes I like to be free.

When I see all the pretty clothes, I think I'm lucky that I'm a girl. But sometimes I want to be a boy because I want to do some of the things boys do—like go hunting and fishing. I know some of the boys at school do the things girls do. My neighbors say that girls and boys are different because girls play with dolls and boys play with trucks.

Around here girls can get jobs in stores, or be a nurse, or run a restaurant, or babysit. I guess there should be more to choose from, so we wouldn't have to go off, say to Indiana, to get a job. There's lots of things I'd like to be, but I can't be them all.

Glenna Halcomb
I am holding flowers in our yard on Big Branch

Ruby Cornett
I asked my sister to take a picture of me on Easter morning

33

Fifth grader
Self-portrait, Cowan Creek

34

Fifth grader
Self-portrait, Cowan Creek

35

Denise Dixon
Self-portrait reaching for the Red Star sky

Denise Dixon
Self-portrait reaching for the Red Star sky

Janet Stallard
I took a picture of myself with the statue in the backyard

Luke Capps
Self-portrait in front of the barn

Animals

Willie Whitaker
The hen

Delbert Shepherd

I put my chickens in a place where they can keep dry. I feed 'em corn and water 'em. I feed the little ones corn bread. I clean out a place where they can run around. Inside the hens is a hen bag that makes eggs everyday. The first time I saw a chicken killed, I felt like it was right sickening for somebody to do that to an animal. It didn't seem right that people wanted to have them around and then kill them, but I've learned it's for food. At first I couldn't eat the animals that I'd seen killed because I was scared. I've learned to try it and if I like it, it's all right, but I just think about somebody killing me. I think of what it must feel like. I think if I were a chicken, after they'd picked all my feathers off, they'd hold a paper bag over me and light it. I'd come out all in pieces—my legs, my neck, back, my breast, ribs, but it helps you to understand the way you're put together, the way God made you.

One of my friends fights chickens alot. He fights big roosters. He buys these roosters that can't stay with another rooster. They think they're the boss, and when he puts two of them together, they try to kill one another to be the winner. Two boys each bet a dollar on one of the roosters. They're professional fighters, just like humans are boxers, but it's more like trying to kill one another—a killing match. They outlawed it because they thought it was being cruel to animals and I think it is.

You watch animals play and all of a sudden it comes naturally to you. You love them. You get attached to them, and you can't separate.

Birds communicate to birds. Dogs communicate to dogs. When a dog barks, it's trying to tell you something. You can't understand it, but a dog understands you. Animals are smart. If they weren't, a cat wouldn't know how to climb a tree. A duck wouldn't know how to swim. Animals are smarter than people. They've lived out in the mountains so long, they know the way. They can go anywhere they want to. People can't. It took years and years for them to discover the wheel.

Animals can find food and protect people from enemies. They can sense danger that we can't. In the dark of the night they sense it, when it's right in front of them. Dad says it's more fun to hunt the animals than it is to kill them. He likes to watch their reactions, how they move. Where there's mountains, there's a lot more animals. They like higher places where hunters can't find them, and they know when you're in the mountains.

Jim Elliott
My mother feeding the cat

Billy Jean Caudill
My dog

45

Robert Gatton
Cats on Halloween

46

Todd Caudill
Our family dog

47

Clifford Brown
Our hunting dogs chained up

Delana Ison
Our cows eating on Cowan Creek

49

Joy Ingram
My daddy is measuring our hog

Susan Cornett
Pig's head killed by my Uncle Woodrow

Ruby Cornett
Daddy at our hog killing, Big Branch

Ruby Cornett

God made animals so that when we got here, they'd be here for us to eat. We've got a cow, and a horse, and two pigs. Mommy usually milks the cow and feeds the horse and the pigs. I have to go with mommy to milk because the cow has horns and mommy's afraid she'll butt her. I stand in the barn door and keep the kittens out of the milk. I go with her every evening and daddy goes with her in the morning.

When we get our hogs real fat, daddy kills them. A hog killing's fun in the winter when it snows. Uncles, aunts, and cousins are there, and friends and neighbors. Most of them sit around and drink beer. Daddy shoots the hog in the head or the neck. It squeals and falls down and dies. The men drag it out of the hog lot and put it on a board and pour boiling water over it and then scrape the hair off of it. I run around with the other girls. We slide in the snow and sit and watch them scrape the hair off, and cut it into pieces. We broil some meat in the fire, and listen to the dogs barking, and the men talking and the fire popping.

Willie Whitaker
My father and his mule

Bill Caudill
My goat on Kingdom Come Creek

Family Portraits

Greg Cornett
Gary Crase and his Mom and Dad in front of their house on Campbells Branch

Gary Crase

I'm the youngest one in my family and just about the youngest in my class. I can take it as it comes and make the best of it when I can. I get up about the same time everyday—fifteen til 7:00. I'm like an alarm clock. I get up and go to bed about the same time. I come back from school and get what lessons I've got and if I have the time, I go to one of the neighbor's houses or down to mamaw's. Down at mamaw's I sit and talk to papaw, and mommy talks to mamaw. I guess girl to girl and boy to boy. Papaw and I talk about the birds, and how his arthritis has been, and have we killed any squirrels lately.

If I had the proper tools, I could take care of myself in the wilderness, and I can think up ways of making things easier. Some people around here call me Albert Einstein. Before there was television in our family we didn't have too much to do—just a few games, and pretty soon it was the same old game over and over, so I started making things. Our family doesn't have a story that's been handed down from generation to generation. I think they came from Canada. My great-grandma was a full blooded Indian. I've got white and black and red and yellow blood mixed into my family, and I'm very proud of it.

Daddy was working at a sawmill and somehow he and my grandpa met. My mom wasn't born then. One day they came up to the sawmill and told grandpa that he'd had a baby girl. Daddy was the only one that had a car, so he took him up to see the baby. He went up there and picked her up in his arms and said, "someday, this is going to be my wife," and

that was the day my mom was born. She got married to daddy when she was fifteen. Back then fifteen was about the right age to get married. Mommy dated other boys. Well, back in those days you stayed at the house and sat out on the front porch and that was a date. Mom was sixteen when she had my sister. Then she waited ten years before she had me. When they first got married they used to live in a house with daddy's mother. Later on they built a one room house sixteen by twenty foot. They had a kitchen, living room, and sleeping part all in one. Later they built two porches and boxed them off, and that made it a three-room house. Then mamaw moved into the house because she had cancer on her left side. She died in the bed daddy sleeps in.

My mother's always had a lot of friends. She had to work hard in her family. Her mother wasn't able to do things, so they mostly depended on her. They had a good time and discarded the worries to her. She's had a real tough life, but she's had good times. She's learned to speak up to people and stand up for what she believes in. She's learned how to survive and how to live on a handful of corn meal. When the world has to come to it again, she'll know how. Things got better for mommy when she married daddy, and they could help each other.

You might say she's the root of the family. She tries to take care of most of the problems, and when something goes wrong, she tries to mend it. She's the chief of the emotions, and when I didn't have a toy, she could always make one.

My sister is 10 years, 7 months, and so many days older than I am. She's the only sister I have, so she's the only person I could be really close to. Ours was a normal brother/sister growing up. Just about anytime we had free time we were together. She's just like my mommy. She's a chip off the old block. She helps people all she can. Gives food to other people before she'll take it herself. She don't complain about many things. She's had a lot of heartbreaks in her life, just about everybody does.

My father does most of the hard work and he brings home the money. He's not a guy you can walk up to and express yourself to, but he's not the hardest guy to live with either. He expects just about the same out of us as we do out of him. He doesn't travel too much, just to the post office, to get the paper, and back to the house. Other people might not like the kind of life we live, and we might not like the life they live. I'd like for my family to have more money, have better housing, better furniture, but we make do. Still there's always laughter in our house, and we look forward to holidays and weekends especially since that's when we got to see my sister because she lives farther away than our legs can walk.

A family is a group of people that has more concern for each other than two friends would have. They share ideals. They share their feelings with each other. When you're part of a family you don't have to go home and talk to the wall. You have somebody that will reply back to you. There's always another person you can turn to. You kind of know where everybody is. You know your daughter lives next door and your cousin lives straight across from you. They visit you a lot. You're with them, and you can talk with them.

There isn't much money here, and you can't find good places to work in. Far off, you can work in big offices and direct people how to do things. Back here you can't find jobs like that, but here you can have all kind of animals, and the good soil raises good crops. In the mountains people usually live close to business. They mine coal, and there's coal mines all over the place. In the city when they go to the office, they have so many things to worry about: files, records, secretaries, and things like that. Out in coal mines you don't have files and secretaries.

There are more dangers in the city than there are in the mountains. From what I have heard, the city is like a chicken house with a fox loose in it. The people are all scattered, and unless the farmer throws the fox out, the chickens can't all group back together. Like here, we have communities. In a way people copy each other. When one gets a red truck, two or three or four gets a red truck. Each family has their own belief. Most people that live together all believe in one general idea like a paragraph in a book. They're all working together to make one general idea come about. It's about the same thing with a community. Maybe one family in a community believes that two and two is three and another one believes that two and two is four, but they both believe that two and two is.

Vernon Gay Cornett
A portrait of my family

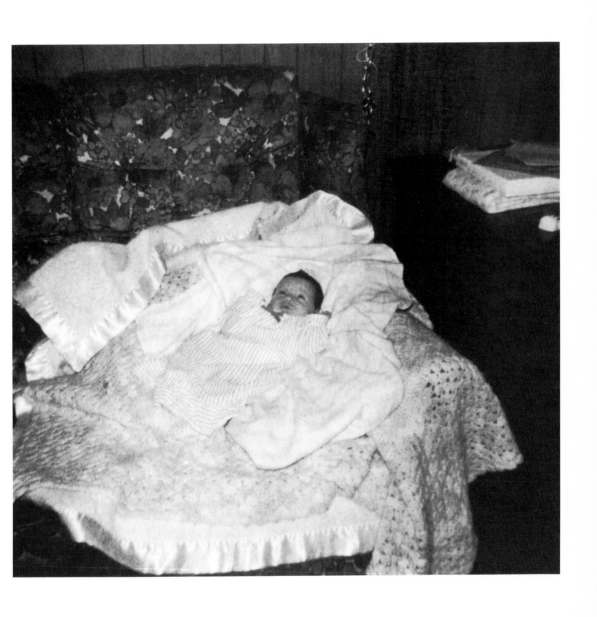

Jerry Ed Ison
My newborn niece

Mary Jo Cornett
My family eating Sunday dinner

Mary Jo Cornett
Mamaw and my sister with the picture of my cousin that died

63

Johnny Wilder
My mother is watching a story

Sixth grader
Mamaw and the baby

Mary Jo Cornett
My brother and sister in the cow barn, Kingdom Come Creek

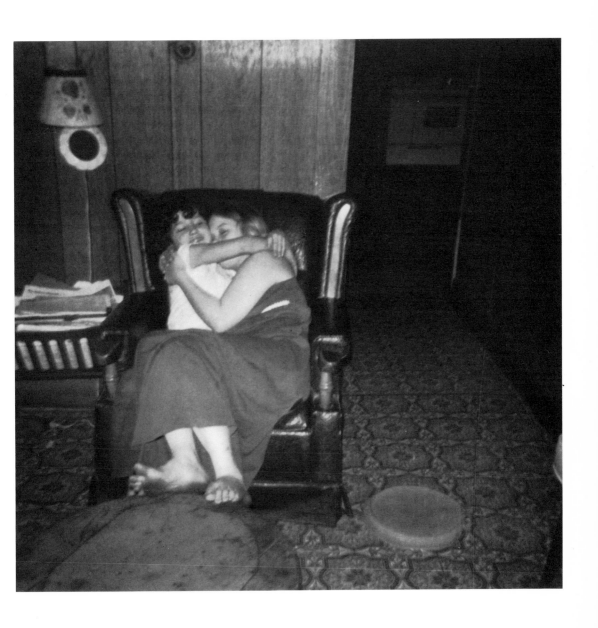

Denise Collins
My cousins

Luke Capps
My sisters playing in the mud

Willie Whitaker
My niece with a .22

Diane Fields
My family in our house on Cowan Creek

Ginnie Walters
My foster family on Turkey Creek

71

Daniel Sexton
My brother and his wife

Daniel Sexton
Mommy and daddy in the kitchen

Martha Campbell
Mommy and daddy

74

Martha Campbell
My older sister holding her baby

Luke Capps
Playing with bikes

Vernon Gay Cornett
Daddy and Eddie and the newborn colt

Joy Ingram
My Daddy feeding the cows

Dewayne Cole

My father grew up in Daisy and my mother grew up on Turkey Creek. They went to school together. My mother's just about like any other mother. She does everything for me. She gets me up every morning and that's hard to do. She cooks for me. Cleans up my bedroom. Fixes me things to eat. I like her a lot. She has brown hair and black eyes. She's fat and short. I'm about as tall as she. I like the way she looks.

Dad works in the coal mines. Mom works in the kitchen and I work at books. My brother Bobby is just in the first grade. He's all the time botherin' you. And I've got one brother that's just in the last year of school and one that's already married. He works in the mines. His wife works in the kitchen and watches TV and listens to the radio, but she cleans up after him. He's a mess.

Our house sure wouldn't be any fun without my mother around, but I'm close to both mom and dad. My dad and I go hunting, work together. We build things. We're making a grease rack now, where he can work on his truck. We just about do everything together. I feel about my mom the same as I feel about my dad. When I have problems, he'll help me. My family works hard. They feel good about it, but they don't like to have to work all the time.

I don't feel too good about my dad working in the mines. It's dangerous. He's been hurt five or six times. A big hook on a cable cut him right through his forehead. He could stick four of his fingers down in under his eye. He stayed in the hospital for two weeks.

My mom doesn't like to talk about my dad getting hurt. My mother thinks sometimes that something's happened to my dad, but if he gets hurt, somebody always comes over and tells us, while they take him on to the hospital. Families here think about each other. They know everybody and every place. Anybody gets hurt and you know about it in a few minutes. News up here goes around fast.

The same old thing, day after day. You don't hardly notice things until they're gone. The mountains are big and I feel good in them. I can go anywhere. Nothing bothers me up there except now they're tearing the mountains up with bulldozers—getting the coal out and making new places for houses. They're destroying them. They've killed almost everything that's up there. I'd like to plant trees and set animals out because soon there won't be anything to look at. It'll just be a plain old place. It makes me sad because I don't like to see anything destroyed, and the people that are destroying it are mostly from the big cities. One man came in here from California. He set the woods on fire because he wanted to burn a big place off where he could set his equipment. I don't like people from the cities. I don't like the way they talk and the way they dress. I just like seeing normal people around.

Delana Ison
Estill Pence, roof bolter, Southeast mine

80

Delana Ison
Moving hoses for the continuous miner at the Southeast Poly Mine

Ruby Cornett
Shift change at the Poly Mine

Ruby Cornett
Miners going home at the end of the shift

Denise Dixon

I had a lot of scary dreams when I was little. I had so many bad dreams, I didn't want to go to sleep at night. They'd just come on. Most of them were about dead people and graves. When my grandmother's mommy died and was laying in her casket, I dreamed that I had to jump over her casket to get to my mother's house because someone was after me. If I have a dream that somebody I know dies, then they usually do die. One time I dreamed there was a baby in a casket. I didn't know whose it was, and one of its eyes was out. The next day, my friend Libby's baby died and they said it had one eye open. If I dream, I dream something bad. If I don't, I don't dream at all.

I always like my aunt's church because they have organs. The music is real good. They clap and tell stories. One story is about a chicken. The devil told him that he would give him something for each one of his feathers, and in the end he gave away all his feathers, and died. He got cold.

Some people go up in front and the priest gives them water and prays for them. He touches their hand and says they're going to be saved. Being saved means you're one of God's children. If you don't ask God to save you, you'll go to hell. Mamaw was saved in church. Then she was baptised. It was kind of happy but sad. It was a real windy day. It was fall, I think, because it was cold. Just the family was there. We were under a bridge. The preacher took her out into the river. She had a white cap on her head and a white dress on. They started preaching. Then they put a cloth over her mouth and dunked her. They said a prayer real quick and raised her back up. She started crying. Then papaw started crying. I think that really changed her. Before she was always singing and acting foolish. She doesn't do that anymore. She's kind of quiet.

Darlene Watts

My uncle died and I went to see him in the funeral home, but it didn't really look like him. He always had his hair parted on one side, and they had it all pushed back to cover up where he'd been shot. The acid from the bullets scattered all over his body. Mommy paid for the flowers and his suit and all that. She had him dressed in dark blue pants and vest and a light blue shirt with little stripes on it and a striped blue tie. She picked him out a gold casket.

The funeral was at Trent's at Delphia. It was so sad that I didn't pay any attention to anything. I just looked at his face. I couldn't go to where they buried him. It was hard enough to see him dead. Mommy told me to hug him, so I could remember him but I couldn't. I was afraid if I kissed him or hugged him, I was going to get him wet with my tears.

Sometimes when I'm in bed, I get lost on dreams. I see him and my grandpaw together and they tell me not to tell mommy I saw them. One day, mommy told me to go in the house and get her something. His picture was sitting on the stereo and when I walked in, I froze. I thought it was really him and he was talking to me. It was like I was dead for a minute talking to him.

I miss my grandpa, more than anybody. He was my favorite person. I might like mommy and daddy and love them, but I loved him better. He said I was his favorite granddaughter. Nobody remembers him quite as well as I do. Me and him was a whole lot alike. That's how I got my brown hair and my brown eyes. He's the one that learned me how to walk. Daddy said he was learning me how to walk as soon as I was born. He said he wanted this grandchild to be special. He made me little houses in the woods, out of tree leaves. He would take his knife, cut off tree limbs and stake them up and make a little hut to stay in. We'd take just what we needed. He'd cut a limb and take the bark off of it and make string, and we'd fish with that, and if we didn't catch nothing, we'd pick berries and eat them for supper. We'd drink from the stream.

I'll say my grandfather is in heaven, because he would sit and read me the Bible every night before we'd go to sleep. He'd always tell me to be a good little girl. He had buried what he thought was important in his life. My grandma said he buried his wedding ring. He was a carpenter, and he buried the first little shelf he made. He said he was saving them for his most loved grandchild and he said that was me. When he died all the grandchildren cried but my grandpa always told me to be brave. He said, "don't cry at my funeral," but I cried anyway. Now when I'm feeling like I should not have cried about something, it seems like he comes down and tells me it's all right. I don't always have to feel guilty. Sometimes I think he's talking to me. I'll want to tell everybody, but it seems like everytime I try to tell it something holds back and won't let go. It's just hard to tell.

I think there'll be a time when no more people are here on earth. I guess it will be when God wants it to be. When I imagine it, in ways it's scary and in other ways, it's good because the land can be free. People won't be tramping on it. The earth can feel the hurt from the way we've used it, but the sad thing is, we won't be here to see the pretty green grass or grow the corn.

Darlene Watts
Singing at the graveyard where my papaw is buried, Memorial Day

Darlene Watts
Some women singing at our church, Cedar Grove

Theresa Eldridge
My sister's baby's funeral

88

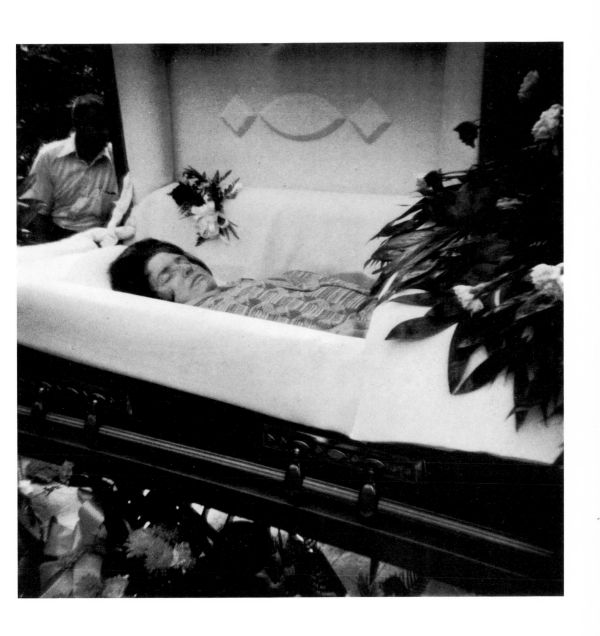

John Morton
My aunt's funeral outside on the lawn

89

Maywood Campbell

My Mamaw and papaw's graves at Christmas time

Darlene Watts
The women hugging after church

Dreams

Wendy Denise Caudill
A dream about my wedding with my brother as the groom

Darlene Watts

I was the first grandchild to be born on my mom's side. My grandpa, just before he died said not to tell any of the other grandchildren, but I was his pick. Sometimes I try to find the biggest piece of paper I can, and I draw me a tree and make me a family tree. I try to go back and find all my uncles and aunts, but it's impossible. I've got some all over the world. Some of them were in the war.

I've gotten lonely before, and I stayed out in the yard and just listened to the birds. Then I imagined that they came down and played with me. I sat there and dreamt all day. I'd imagine there were bears that lived around here that would come down and play with me, and deer. It seems they were real people and they found the best clothes they could to wear. The bluebirds found the best color of blue. We played and drank tea. I talked like them. The bears would tell me to get some fish and I would go fishing and get them some fish. The birds would want bird seed and I would get them some bird seed. I was a genie. They would wish for something and I would give it to them.

Mommy says I imagine too much sometimes. Maybe I lose my mind. I like to imagine because I think someday it'll come true. My mom always dreamed of having a house of her own. Now she's about got it. She imagined to always have an older girl and a younger son, and she's got us. I think if you don't have an imagination, you don't have a life.

To dream some of the dreams I've dreamed my mind has to be five or six times as big as the world. There are different places in my mind. And it's just full of a bunch of machines making it go.

Sometimes when my friends are mad at me, daydreaming makes me feel less lonely. Makes me feel like I've got somebody there to talk to. One time when I was at one of my friend's houses, she begged me to stay. I didn't want to, but I thought I'd stay so she wouldn't be mad at me, and just think about something else. So I thought that I was standing in the corner of the world where I could reach everything and I could make everything happen like I wanted it to happen. The farmers that wanted rain for their crops, I made it rain in that certain spot. If one city didn't have electricity, I gave it electricity. All the people that didn't have food or clothes, I let them go into the store and get what they wanted and needed. Everybody had their own way, and by the time I got through with everybody, I couldn't think any more. I was asleep.

If I could change anything I wanted, first of all, I'd make my family better, so they wouldn't be sick anymore. Maybe I could get mommy some new clothes. She says all she has is rags. I'd get them a cooker, and a screwdriver, and a little ball for Christmas. I'd change a lot I guess. I'd change mommy's dreams. I'd give her a brick house with lots of green grass in the yard, and I'd like to make my dad's dreams come true. He'd like to have hogs and have his hog pen built and have a new driveway.

My father just works in the coal mines. He works real hard. Sometimes I think he needs a little bit more rest. He's sort of sick himself. He'd rather just go on and forget about his health and just worry about ours. Me and mommy and Tommy try to tell him his life is worth a lot to us too, but he says we come first. I worry about all my family because they're all sick in some way.

I wish a lot of things would change —like dying, and I wish Dad would never die, never get old. Sometimes I wish I wasn't born, but then I wouldn't be here talking, and I'm kind of glad I'm here talking.

Denise Dixon
A dream about my doll

96

Denise Dixon
I am Dolly Parton

Lisa Gray
My cousin on Christmas

Gwen Trent
My sister with her pinwheel

Denise Dixon
Phillip and Jamie doing somersaults

100

Denise Collins
My little sister and my dolls

Allen Shepherd
I dreamt I killed my best friend, Ricky Dixon

Mike Stallard
Self-portrait as a monster

Scott Huff
My space ship was taking off
A flying dream. My parachute landed in a tree

104

Scott Huff
The planes were crashing on my head

Sue Dixon
A dream of falling

Ruby Cornett
Self-portrait in a dream about floating

Denise Dixon
My brother the mud monster

108

Denise Dixon
My brother the mud monster

109

Denise Dixon
I dreamt the twins tried to kill each other
Phillip was supposed to be dead but Jamie sees him floating in the trees

Denise Dixon
I dreamt the twins tried to kill each other
Phillip is a witch. Jamie has to kill him by driving a stake into his heart

111

Denise Dixon
I dreamt the twins tried to kill each other

Denise Dixon
Jamie is praying for help from his kin people who have died

113

Denise Dixon

I like to take pictures from my dreams, from television, or just from my imagination. I like those kind of pictures because they're scary. If I didn't know how I took them, I'd be scared by them. My twin brothers, Phillip and Jamie, pose for me. Sometimes they're good at having their pictures taken, but they get tired of it.

I made a long dream with Phillip and Jamie which comes from TV shows I've watched. I told Jamie to lay down and then I put all this makeup on him to make scars and scratches on his mouth down through his nose and on his hands. I put wood on top of him like a house fell on him, and I told him to act like he was dead. I took some in the graveyard above my house. For one I told Jamie to grab a hold of the gravestone and start screaming. For the other I told him to kneel down. I told him to bow down like he was sad. I took the picture from the foot of the grave that had just been filled.

I always think about what I'm going to do before I take the picture. I have taken pictures of myself as Dolly Parton and Marilyn Monroe and then there was the girl with the snake around her neck. She was supposed to be a movie star, but really it was me. For some I was dancing in my bathing suit while the music was playing in the basement. I told my girlfriend, Michelle, how far away to stand and to take the pictures when I said. I like people in action, and I always look for a certain time to take a picture.

Denise Dixon
Phillip and Jamie are creatures from outer space in their space ship

Afterword

Ben Lifson

These are photographs by children from the hollers of Letcher County, Kentucky. Children familiar with mountains and woods and the ways of the small animals they hunt there with their .22s, children familiar with strip mines and shaft mines and deaths by mining accidents, black lung, fratricide and suicide. Wendy Ewald, who taught them how to photograph, says that they also knew the name of every house and path and notch in the mountains, of almost every stone or tree or creek bend or abandoned cabin site old enough or vivid enough to have a name.

They were unfamiliar with the traditions of either portraiture or the genre scene in either painting or photography. Those who had taken art lessons in school had been asked no more than to copy pictures from books. From Ewald they learned pictorial clarity and emphasis. She taught them the differences between perception, sight and camera vision (although she did not use those words) and they learned to photograph in terms of the latter. Ewald showed them how to create many special effects both with the camera and in the darkroom. The children rejected these techniques as uninteresting novelties. They were after a blunt and naked presentation of subject, a photography unembellished and direct.

Although they were children, they seldom photographed from below; they stood level with their subjects, that is, they avoided distortion. They rarely estheticized their subjects, picturing things as fragments or as shapes. The light in their photographs is not often dramatic; be it the wan light of short Appalachian winters without snow or the lush summer sunlight falling into the hollers between dark mountains, it is depicted matter-of-factly, as a property of time and place.

Ewald tells us that her students were among the first generation of Appalachian children who did not have to go to work in the fields or mines at an early age. They had time to notice things simply for the sake of it. Russell Akeman photographed "just to be doing." It was a pleasure, along with "work in the garden, plowing, tilling and all the grass. Maybe drink Kool-Aid. . . . I can work all day and not quit." He could expose two to three rolls of film every afternoon in the half hour or so before sunset, his favorite time. "I take enough of them," he said.

Out of this kind of pleasure come photographs that are to the ambitious photographer what good common letters and journals are to the ambitious writer: easy natural productions that make one long to work without self-consciousness. And although we know the children to have been skilled and disciplined, they photographed as children looked at things, as though for the first time, with a gaze neither dispassionate nor moved, neither rude nor ceremonious, neither magisterial nor naïve but simply curious and engaged. They seem to have walked up to their subjects and to have stopped when they saw them clearly and whole. In every instance we feel that they took the problem of where to put the camera as a fresh one. Hence the extraordinary variety of picture structure within what is essentially a group style.

Here a baby and her blankets fill the lower half of the frame as if welling up in the center of it and flowing down to its edges. There chained hounds in a bright backyard, photographed from afar, stretch and take their places as small and distant figures in the serene classical order of the scene. Delana Ison, looking through a wire fence at two calves eating in their pen, used the blurred horizontals and verticals of the fence wire as a grid to compose the scene. It is satisfying to be shown one thing at a time, the sloping roof of the shed, the battered pail; and to be led along the white strips of hide on the calves' backs and down to where the calves' necks seem to merge and the two heads become clear variations on the same shape. That the calves don't astonish or amuse us as some animals do in photographs is not important. They inspired a still attentiveness in Delana Ison and led her to a precise delineation of the differences contained within a routine backyard sight, and it is enough for anyone to see and to express herself so clearly.

Asked why she had included so much of a cinderblock wall in photographs of herself wearing a bathing suit and reaching heavenwards, Denise Dixon explained, "I was supposed to be dancing. . . . See, the music was in that basement, and [the camera] was right beside the basement." From blitheness in relation to what can be photographed (a wall) and what can't (music) come bold effects like Dixon's description of the wall itself, massive, raking and mottled. Amateur photographers don't include such things, and ambitious photographers attempt them warily. Dixon's wall therefore strikes us as a risk stemming from an impulse, from an energy allowed to go slightly out of control, even though Dixon herself did not intend it so.

In leaving the children free to choose for themselves what to photograph Ewald shares a belief with the New Zealand novelist and teacher Sylvia Ashton-Warner: that children can become eloquent in an unfamiliar medium if they are asked to tell us about what they know intimately and about what crucially affects them. "Children have two visions," Ashton-Warner writes, "the inner and the outer. Of the two the inner vision is the brighter."* Ashton-Warner asked her five-year-old Maori students to tell her the words they wanted to learn. They were invariably words relating to

*Ashton-Warner, Sylvia. *Teacher*, Simon & Schuster, New York, 1963. Page 32 *et passim*.

sex and fear: "kiss," "skeleton," "knife," "Mummy," "Daddy," "hit," "darling," "beer." From this "key vocabulary" the children themselves made the first English sentences they learned to read and write: "Mummie got a hiding off Daddy. He was drunk. She was crying." "Our baby is dead. She was dead on Monday night. When mummie got it." "I went to the river and I kissed Lily and I ran away. Then I kissed Philliaa. Then I ran away and went for a swim" – sentences and stories Ashton-Warner calls the "captions" of pictures within the child's mind: ". . . adult chosen pictures can be meaningful and delightful to children, but it is the captions of the mind pictures that have the power and the light." Now, to some degree Ewald's students photographed according to "adult chosen pictures," for they were photographing according to a kind of picture they knew well, the portraits and the scenes that one finds in family snapshot albums. But they were photographing each other and themselves. Said another way, they were *posing* for each other and for themselves. Some girls affect looks of sentimental longing; one poses with her brother's rifle; serene, almost regal Glenna Halcomb sits on a small mound of earth in her front yard holding a sprig of flowering branches. An armed boy stands guard over a white rabbit, another poses on his tricycle in a rubber Hallowe'en fright mask. A small girl marches through a living room in self-conscious majesty holding a bright plastic pinwheel. Another holds a doll to her chest as though mothering it, even though the vinyl jacket she wears – a Christmas present – is so stylish that we know she is almost too old for dolls. These are not the poses children strike for adults. At least, I cannot name offhand the culture whose routine Easter Morning snapshots – taken by adults – show children posing as Ruby Cornett poses here: in her bathrobe in the backyard, with an inflatable plastic Easter Bunny in the leafless sapling next to her. We sense that these pictures, are versions of the children's inner pictures of themselves, illustrations of unconscious texts.

What vision of herself did Ruby Cornett give us when she posed that Easter Morning? Some texts we will never recover. Others, like six-year-old Freddy Childers's, seem more accessible. The first time Freddy took a camera home he photographed himself posing with his mentally retarded brother Homer. Then he photographed himself holding a portrait of his dead brother Everett. We hesitate to name the connections he might have felt between the one act and the other lest we blur the delicate map of sorrow, memory, love and hope that is sketched simply and elegantly when the two pictures are seen together. However, we must point out Freddy's tact. With Homer he smiles lightly; with the photograph of Everett he grieves.

Many of the pictures in this volume are already in the children's family albums. To the children and their families over the years they will summon up associations, details and stories – a continuously self-revising stream of captions. We can only read the laconic literal titles here – "My daddy feeding the cows," "My foster family on Turkey Creek," "My mother feeding the cat," "My sister's baby's funeral," "Mamaw and the baby" – repeat the words, and point to the beauties of the photographs. But in many cases, if we take the captions away we are speechless, as if in the presence of a mystery.

Consider Darlene Watts's two pictures of women in a darkened room. In one the women stand, hold themselves, and watch; in the other they embrace. What vigil is described? What greeting? What spectacle have the women come to witness? What disturbance has come to the community, driving the women to this dark place at night to seek comfort in each other's arms? The captions tell us that the women are singing at church and hugging after a church service. But to know this does not explain why the women hold themselves so tightly, or why one agitated woman moves in anger. Nor do we know why, when they embrace, the women look about them with such anxiety. Without captions we are left to contemplate the emotion, and the thick and rigid bodies, studies in human form.

I write "studies" appealing to its usage in art. Considered as pictures without titles, many of the works here strike us as explorations (or *études*) of their subjects, pictures of things seen, arrested and held up for contemplation – not reports but fantasies, and not literary fantasies but visual ones, variations on a motif, especially on the motif of the human figure, figures which are often strange, slightly off, yet rendered with such apparent precision and control that, while they are clearly photographic transcriptions of appearances, they have the singularity and surprise of quick, sure inventions of the artist's hand, improvisations, drawings, not observations of what the body looked like but proposals for what it might look like, and as such they seem to spring from the children's visual imagination.

In some of the most fantastic pictures here children hang upside down from trees, from sheds, and from ledges in the hills. The captions tell us that these pictures represent episodes from dreams – the most private texts and visions that Ewald asked her pupils to illustrate.

These are scenes of flying, of falling, of floating, of being pursued by creatures from outer space, of being attacked by toys or captured by dolls and absorbed into their world; of killing one's best friend, of watching one twin kill another and be haunted by his ghost. To see Wendy Denise Caudill pose as a bride with her kid brother as her groom, to see Denise Dixon's naked mud-daubed brother pose spread legged and close to the lens is to have the sensation that we look directly into the photographers' unconscious wishes.

"I dreamed I killed my best friend Ricky Dixon," writes Allen Shepherd. In Shepherd's picture a boy, his face pale with winter light, his eyes closed, slumps forward as if hit from behind, and falls into the fork of a large tree. His arms are outspread. His body is in the crotch of the tree, as if between two thick legs. We can read the picture in terms of birth and sex and crucifixion – pictures as deep in the unconscious as murder, yet perhaps not retrievable to Allen Shepherd because not admissible, although present enough to us.

And if you look hard at Ricky Dixon's face or at the face of Scott Huff in his flying dreams, or at Denise Dixon's little brother as he holds the tombstone and screams in the vampire dream or at the girls who fall and float, you will see emotions – lusts and fears – that are broader than either the picture or the caption warrants, nameless, and elemental.

And they are not that much more exaggerated than the anxious looks on the faces of the women in church, or than the grin on the face of a butcher with a severed hog's head. Visually, the line between the dream pictures, and the portraits and the photographs of daily life, is thin. The miracle of these photographs is that while the children map their inner worlds they are also our guides to the material culture and daily and occasional life of the hollers. They teach us how hogs are measured before slaughter, and show us that graves are decorated at Christmas, that at one funeral, at least, the open casket lay for viewing on the lawn outside the church, and that on solemn occasions men and women customarily and calmly hold their folded hands at their waists – and that posing for a photograph is considered a solemnity, so often is that gesture seen in portraits.

As this inventory grows we understand the children's work as a collective document and communal history, and the children as the hollers' chroniclers and scribes.

There can be little doubt that they understood photographs as chapters of family history, artifacts uniting the generations. Photographs of the absent were understood as presences: In Diane Fields's picture of her family there is a framed portrait of Fields herself, who put it there so that she too would be present in the family group.

There is no doubt that the children knew themselves to be making documents. At the beginning of her teaching, Ewald asked the children to photograph a day at school as an exercise in analyzing, expressing and recording something at once so complicated, public and objective. In 1977, when the children were preparing the work for exhibition in Chicago and New York, they decided that they had to photograph the mines and the land the better "to explain" the place to outsiders.

Yet how public a sense of the documentary did they have? They were not primarily interested in the structure of communal life. They scarcely examined their families' relationships, much less their fathers' and mothers' friendships. They did not photograph the towns or the roads connecting them; nor did they photograph stores, gas stations or other places where people gather, except for church.

Their world is intimate and still. The places they describe are self-contained and proportionate; no fragments of details along the edges of the pictures imply connection to a larger world just outside the frame. Here time is slow, bound to custom and the change of seasons. Parents are affectionate but not sexual. From where the children stand adults seem large even when they are not so near. Dolls and pets are close but not larger than life. Where backyards merge with saplings and underbrush the small and knowable thinly wooded foothills still look like forest, and beckon. The children see three stages of human life – childhood, adulthood and old age. They do not photograph adolescence – indeed, every one of them stopped taking pictures at puberty – thus the time that most immediately awaits them is held at bay, and the pace of this work seems slower still. Depicting neither advertising signs nor automobiles, and giving cursory description of mass-produced objects (ready-made clothing, for example) whose style would summarize the times, this collective document is largely dateless. The moments it describes occur in emotional not historical time. The children's Letcher County has something of the remoteness of myth or of those ballads whose action occurs in a far country ruled by a nameless lord.

Yet how full their realm is of life's clutter and informality: a coffee cup left precariously on the back of a couch; untied sneakers; awkward kisses. When Ginnie Walters photographed "My Foster Family on Turkey Creek" early in the morning, her little sister stands in the dusty yard still wearing her white fluffy bedroom slippers. We feel that we are in the hands of good photographers because they keep surprising us. Their appetite for pictures and for the way things look in pictures is large and delights us. As they lead us to what is beautiful in the commonplace we accept them as trustworthy guides to the hollers, and they enlarge our sense of what a document can contain. To take a stance that says "These things must be photographed – preserved and remembered" is to act, intentionally or not, as the conscience of a community.

The driving conscience of this work is Wendy Ewald's. She believed that if left to follow their hearts and pleasures, the children would show us both what they cherished and what their community holds dear. She confirmed them in their preference for the plainest of photographic styles, knowing that such a style would lend the authority of the document even to incidental background – descriptions of dishes neatly stacked in glass-doored cupboards and to sunlight splashing in through a screen door – rudimentary cameras and darkrooms not withstanding. Choosing the pictures for this book she realized the Letcher County latent in the projects of dozens of children. She realized the Photography in their individual performances and gave it integrity.

In truth, much of the richness, variety, density, and surprise and a great deal of what we accept as the children's grave and precocious sense of purpose came about not because Ewald gave her students a sense of mission but because she asked them to photograph their dreams. Scott Huff, wanting to represent a spaceship from his dreams, photographed his family's heating-oil tank. Ruby Cornett went to a place she knew in the woods, a ledge on a steep hill, and there pretended to float as in a dream. Although playing dress-up is central to childhood, Wendy Denise Caudill photographed herself in a wedding gown and her little brother in a man's hat only because "I dreamed I got married and my brother was the groom." Playgrounds, picnic tables, swing sets, tricycles, front steps and other common things are photographed not for themselves but as the settings and props of dreams.

And so we see to what uses a child's imagination puts the sights of daily life. Consider the dream pictures as illustrations of dream texts. In children's books young heroes and heroines wish themselves to hidden gardens, exotic jungles and castles in the clouds, and the illustrations literally take them there. But in Letcher County children fly by dangling upside down from the roof of the shed. Visitors from outer space, their helmets resembling nothing less than nylon stockings pulled over their heads, their spaceship a family arm chair, sit and wriggle their naked toes. This is the stuff of children's play – the moment that the little brother becomes the vampire and a piece of lath becomes the stake through his heart, and yet he remains a little boy in a hooded sweatshirt and the lath only lies on his chest. These children have photographed those moments so plainly that we can say that their dreams and fantasies have not been *imitated* but *documented*.

Documentary photographs are an arm of memory. And these clear depictions of children's yearnings to be heroic, desirable, adult, to hunt with a brother's rifle or to take a brother in wedlock are worth remembering. Part of their culture's desire, they fade when the dreamer reaches puberty. Pictures here of the children's parents, tired, listless, overweight – the future toward which the children move – make it clear that these childhood visions of giving oneself over to sun and mud and earth and forest, of beautiful and strange animals appearing to them everywhere, of visitors from outer space sitting in their family's living rooms, that these records of a summery imagination must be preserved lest the children forget them when adult and thus forget the consummation that they dreamed of. Who among you does not wish that you could recall better what you imagined when you were young, or what the world looked like, or what you wore, when you imagined it?

65. A